and Times

John Philip Sousa

The King of March Music

Jennifer Blizin Gillis

Heinemann Library
Chicago, Illinois

Designed by Lucy Owen and Bridge Creative Services
Originated by Modern Age Repro
Printed and bound by South China Printing Company

10 09 08 07 06
10 9 8 7 6 5 4 3 2 1

Library of Congress Cataloging-in-Publication Data
Gillis, Jennifer Blizin, 1950-
  John Philip Sousa : the king of march music / Jennifer
Blizin Gillis.
      p. cm. -- (Lives and times)
  Includes bibliographical references and index.
  ISBN 1-4034-6751-X (library binding-hardcover)
  1. Sousa, John Philip, 1854-1932--Juvenile literature. 2.
Composers--United States--Biography--Juvenile
literature. I. Title. II. Series: Lives and times (Des
Plaines, Ill.)
  ML3930.S7G55 2005
  784.8'4'092--dc22

                    2005001498

Acknowledgments
The author and publishers are grateful to the following
for permission to reproduce copyright material:
Alamy/Popperfoto p. **4**; Alamy/Sue Cunningham p. **5**;
Corbis pp. **9**, **15**, **16**; Corbis/Bettmann pp. **7**, **13**, **18**, **19**;
Corbis/Bob Rowan/Progressive Image p. **14**;
Corbis/James L. Amos p. **26**; Corbis/Joseph
Sohm/Visions of America p. **27**; Corbis/Lake County
Museum p. **22**; John Philip Sousa: American
Phenomenon by Paul E. Bierley, source unlisted pp. **11**,
23; Lebrecht Music Collection p. **8**; Peter Newark's
Americana Pictures p. **12**; Sousa Archives and Center
for American Music pp. **10**, **21**; The Library of Congress
pp. **6**, **17**, **24**, **25**; The Library of Congress/Defense
Department p. **20**.

Cover photograph of John Philip Sousa reproduced with
permission of Corbis. Photograph of music manuscript
reproduced with permission of Corbis.

Page icons by Corbis

Photo research by Maria Joannou and Virginia
Stroud-Lewis

Every effort has been made to contact copyright
holders of any material reproduced in this book.
Any omissions will be rectified in subsequent
printings if notice is given to the publishers.

Contents

Some words are shown in bold, **like this**. You can find out what they mean by looking in the glossary.

The King of March Music

John Philip Sousa was a famous **composer** and bandleader. He made march music popular all around the world. His "Stars and Stripes Forever" is the national march of the United States.

This is a picture of John during the 1900s.

John **invented** the sousaphone. It is a tuba that wraps around a player's body.

John worked hard all his life. If he had problems, he did not give up. He wrote hundreds of tunes. He wrote music for plays called "operettas." He also wrote seven books.

Musical Childhood

John was born November 6, 1854, in Washington, D.C. John's father came from Spain. He played trombone in the United States **Marine** Band. John's mother came from a country called Bavaria.

John's parents were named John Antonio and Maria Elisabeth.

This is a picture of Washington, D.C. at the time John lived there.

John did not start school until he was seven. He started taking music lessons, too. He learned to play violin, piano, flute, trombone, and a kind of horn called the cornet.

A Young Marine

John was allowed to practice with the **Marine** Band. He started an **orchestra** when he was eleven. John's orchestra played at dancing schools.

John played in an orchestra like this one. The other people in his orchestra were adults.

In John's time, it was not unusual for young boys to join the **military**.

When John was thirteen, a circus bandleader heard him play the violin. He wanted John to join the circus band. John's father was not happy. He made John join the **marines** instead.

John and Jennie

John **published** his first march when he was 19. Two years later he left the **marines**. He went to Philadelphia, Pennsylvania. He got a job playing violin in an **orchestra**.

This is a picture of John when he was 19 years old.

John met an actress when he was 24.
Her name was Jane Bellis. John called her
Jennie. They married in December 1879.

This is a picture of Jennie Bellis.

Good News

When John was 25, he got some good news. The **Marine** Band wanted him as their leader. But the band did not sound very good. John had to get new **musicians**, new instruments, and new music.

John led the Marine Band for twelve years.

12

The new Marine Band played at the White House on New Year's Day in 1881. People loved them! After that, the band played at the White House every Saturday afternoon. Thousands of people came to listen.

While John was the bandleader, the Marine Band became known as the best **military** band in the world.

Marine Band Years

John wrote new marches for the **Marine** Band. One was called "**Semper Fidelis**." It is named after the U.S. Marines' **motto**. John's march became the official march of the U.S. Marines.

The Marine Band still plays John's marches today.

John wrote music in his spare time.

People all over the United States wanted to see the Marine Band. John took the band on a **tour** of the country. But soon he decided to start his own band.

15

The Sousa Band

John's new band was called the Sousa Band. They often played two times a day, seven days a week. They **toured** all over the United States. John's family went with them.

John wrote many new marches for the Sousa Band.

John took his family to Europe for a vacation. On the way home, he heard a march playing in his head. He wrote it down. It became his most famous march.

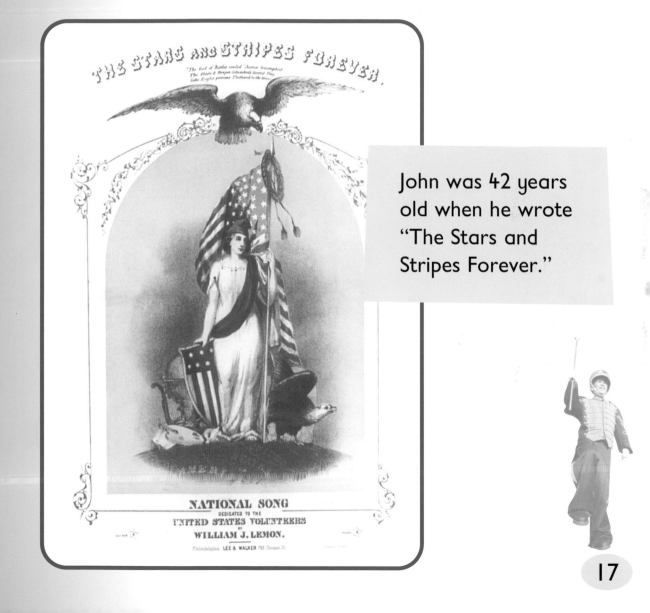

John was 42 years old when he wrote "The Stars and Stripes Forever."

War!

When John was 43 years old the **Spanish-American War** broke out. John wanted to join the **marines** again. Instead he got sick. When he got well, the war was over!

Many people celebrated in New York at the end of the war. The Sousa Band marched there, too.

The King of England gave John a medal in 1901. John was proud to wear his medals.

After the war the Sousa Band started **touring** again. They traveled around the world. They played a new kind of music called **ragtime**. The band was very popular in England and France.

Slowing Down

After **World War I**, John started up the Sousa Band again. They were still very popular. But John was getting old. He could not take the band on long **tours** anymore.

Every summer the Sousa Band played for tourists in Atlantic City, New Jersey.

At that time radio had just been **invented**. The Sousa Band began playing on the radio every week. Thousands of people could hear them at one time. John became even more famous without having to travel.

John was proud of his time in the Navy, so after World War I he usually wore his uniform.

Last Years

Late in life John worked with children. He gave prizes to school bands and **orchestras**. He invited them to play at Sousa Band concerts. He gave money to a summer camp for school band **musicians**.

This picture shows John late in life with Jennie and their daughter, Jane.

This is John's grave at the Congressional Cemetery in Washington, D.C.

John did not want to stop working. But he did not write much music as he got older. On March 6, 1932, he had a heart attack and died.

Learning More About Sousa

Many people wanted to honor John. There are schools, bridges, ships, and fountains named for John Philip Sousa. There is also a concert hall named for John in Washington, D.C.

Each year, school band students can win an award named for John Philip Sousa.

Marching bands everywhere still play John's music. Every July 4, Americans celebrate their country's **independence**. As a band plays "Stars and Stripes Forever," fireworks light up the night sky.

People can hear John's marches at Fourth of July fireworks shows like this one. John's music lives!

Fact File

- John and Jennie had three children. They were called John Philip Sousa Jr., Jane, and Helen.

- John wore white gloves so that **musicians** could see his hands when he led them. He only wore each pair one time. He gave them away to people as presents.

- John loved baseball. The Sousa Band had its own baseball team. John was pitcher.

- John loved to ride horses. In 1921, he fell from a horse and hurt himself. He had a hard time moving his left arm after that.

- John wrote 137 marches and more than 150 other kinds of music during his life.

- John was the oldest man to join the **Navy** in 1917. He worked for only $1 a month.

- At a time when women had few rights, John hired many women **soloists** for his band.

Timeline

1854	John is born on November 6
1867	John's father signs him up for the **Marines**
1872	John **publishes** his first music
1873	John publishes his first march
1875	John leaves the Marines
1879	John marries Jennie Bellis
1880	John becomes leader of the Marine Band
1888	John writes "**Semper Fidelis**"
1892	John starts the Sousa Band
1896	John writes "Stars and Stripes Forever"
1917	John joins the Navy during **World War I**
1929	The Sousa Band begins playing on the radio
1932	John has a heart attack and dies on March 6

Glossary

composer person who makes up music

independence not being controlled by another country

invent to have the idea for a new thing

marines one part of the United States military

military having to do with the army, navy, air force, or marines

motto saying used by a group of people

musician someone who plays music

navy part of the United States military that keeps the ocean safe

orchestra musical group that contains many different instruments

publish have something printed so that it can be sold to other people

ragtime kind of music that has an unusual, or "ragged" beat

Semper Fidelis this means "always faithful." It is the motto of the United States Marines.

soloist person who has a special part playing or singing by him or herself

Spanish-American War war fought in 1899 between the United States and Spain

tour long trip with stops at different places along the way

World War I war that lasted from 1914 to 1918. It involved many countries. The United States joined in 1917.

Find Out More

More Books to Read

Greene, Carol. *John Philip Sousa, The March King.* Chicago, Ill.: Children's Press, 1992.

Venezia, Mike. *John Philip Sousa.* New York, N.Y.: Scholastic, 1999.

Zannos, Susan: *The Life and Times of John Philip Sousa.* Hockessin, Del.: Mitchell Lane, 2003.

Places to Visit

You can find out about John Philip Sousa at:

The Sousa Archives and Center for
   American Music
236 Harding Band Building
1103 South Sixth Street
Champaign, IL 61820
(217) 244-9309

You can contact the Marine Band at:

"The President's Own" U.S. Marine Band
Marine Barracks
8th and I Streets, S.E.
Washington, D.C. 20390
(202) 433-4011

Index